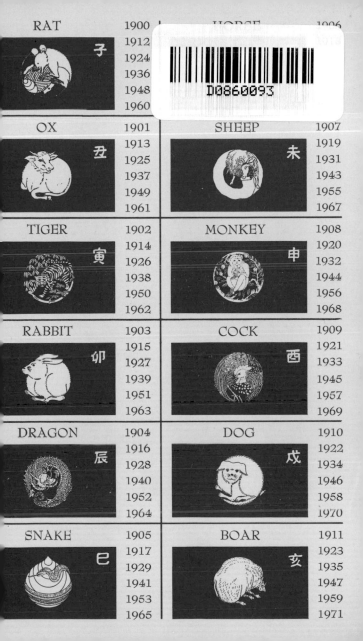

RAT 子	1900	HORSE	1906
	1912		1918
	1924		
	1936		
	1948	D0860093	
	1960		
OX 丑	1901	SHEEP 未	1907
	1913		1919
	1925		1931
	1937		1943
	1949		1955
	1961		1967
TIGER 寅	1902	MONKEY 申	1908
	1914		1920
	1926		1932
	1938		1944
	1950		1956
	1962		1968
RABBIT 卯	1903	COCK 酉	1909
	1915		1921
	1927		1933
	1939		1945
	1951		1957
	1963		1969
DRAGON 辰	1904	DOG 戌	1910
	1916		1922
	1928		1934
	1940		1946
	1952		1958
	1964		1970
SNAKE 巳	1905	BOAR 亥	1911
	1917		1923
	1929		1935
	1941		1947
	1953		1959
	1965		1971

THE JAPANESE
FORTUNE
CALENDAR

by Reiko Chiba

午
未
巳
申
辰
酉
卯
十二支
戌
寅
亥
丑
子

CHARLES E. TUTTLE COMPANY
Rutland, Vermont & Tokyo, Japan

Representatives

For the British Isles & Continental Europe:
SIMON & SCHUSTER INTERNATIONAL GROUP, London

For Australasia:
BOOKWISE INTERNATIONAL
1 Jeanes Street, Beverley, 5009, South Australia

Published by the Charles E. Tuttle Company, Inc.
of Rutland, Vermont and Tokyo, Japan
with editorial offices at Suido, 1-chome, 2–6,
Bunkyo-ku, Tokyo, Japan

Library of Congress Catalog Card No. 65–12970
International Standard Book No. 0–8048–0300–5
First edition, 1965
Thirty-second printing, 1987

Printed in Japan

INTRODUCTION

L IKE people of the West, Eastern people have a zodiac. Unlike that of the West, however, the Eastern system has a cycle of twelve years instead of months. Each year of the cycle has its own particular animal symbol whose roots of meaning, origin, and influence stretch back to ancient India and China.

One of the traditional Japanese stories pertaining to this zodiacal system and how it started runs as follows. On a certain New Year's Day, ages ago, Buddha called all the animals of the world to him. He promised that those who came to pay him homage would receive a gift for their fealty. As a mark of honor, they would be given a year which would thereafter be named for them. Of all the animals in the world, only these twelve came, and they came in this order: the rat and the ox, the tiger and the rabbit, the dragon, the snake, and the horse, the sheep and the monkey, the cock, the dog, and the boar.

When each animal received its year, each contributed its characteristic traits to that year, making the year distinctly its own. According to Japanese belief, people born in one of the cycle's years will have those characteristic traits peculiar to the year's animal.

From these twelve zodiacal symbols a person's fortune may be told. His character index may be gauged, and his strength and weaknesses may be known. What are his talents and how may he use them? What are his limits and how may he recognize them? These questions and their answers, answers for good or ill, are based upon the knowledge of when a person was born; and the elements of that person's birth year, coupled with the understanding of those elements, will determine the course of his or her life, socially, personally, and, in Japan, to some extent even politically.

There are three phases in a person's life span, and the fortune of each phase is clearly defined. Japanese fortune-tellers say that they are able to determine the events for all of these phases and advise or counsel alternative courses to avoid misfortune.

People born in one year may have the characteristics and traits belonging to those born in another. This is not at all unusual. Allowances must be made for those traits peculiar to the individual.

The order in which the animals appear in all cycles is always the same. The animals, as we have noted, are: rat, ox, tiger, rabbit, dragon, snake, horse, sheep, monkey, cock, dog, and boar. As with any of the preceding cycles, the first year of the present cycle began with the year of the rat in 1960. The cycle will end in 1971, the year of the boar. The new cycle will begin in 1972, and it will start, again, with the year of the rat.

Serving as a guide, the end pages of this book have six cycles of the Japanese Fortune Calendar dating from 1900 to 1971. The animal years are in their proper sequence, and the standard calendar years on which they fall are listed. To discover your animal year, count backward from this present year in reverse order of the animal-year sequence, to the year of your birth. If you were born in 1928, for example, and this is 1965, the year of the snake, you would count: snake, dragon, rabbit, tiger, ox, rat, boar, etc., etc. backward until you reached your birth year, which would be the year of the dragon.

Coincidentally and conveniently enough, the 1900's started with the year of the rat. If you wish to count forward from the year 1900 to your birth year, you may find it easier. The Japanese find it easier for them to count from the present year back.

CONTENTS

THE YEAR OF THE RAT

P EOPLE born in the year of the rat are noted for their charm. However, they are fussy about small matters and have a tendency to pinch pennies. When such people want something very much, they will work hard for the thing desired. Because they are thrifty, they are able to save a great deal of money. Unfortunately, they may lose what they have saved by spending it on someone they love who does not love them. Curiously enough, only through love does a person born in this year become generous.

Although people born in this year can maintain an outward show of control, they are easily angered. Their value lies in the fact that they are able to control their discontent or anger. Small-minded as these people are, they are quite honest and ambitious and have a tremendous capacity for pursuing a course to its end. They love to spend money on themselves, denying themselves nothing, but they don't lend. They love to gossip, and because of this characteristic they are apt to have short-term friends.

They will have good fortune in the first phase of their life. But in the second phase they will lose everything they have at one time through a mistakenly taken chance or a shattering love affair. Yet in the latter part of their life they will live well and comfortably.

A person born in the year of the rat would do well to marry someone born in either the dragon, the monkey, or the ox year, for people of these years are temperamentally suited to those of the rat year. The next best choice would be one born in the year of the rat, tiger, snake, dog, or boar. The worst would be with one born in the horse year, and it would be doubly disastrous for a rat-year man to marry a woman born in the year called the "fire horse year," which comes every sixty years. A popular superstition claims that a man marrying such a woman does not live out his full span of life.

THE YEAR OF THE OX

PEOPLE born in the year of the ox are very patient and speak little. They have a gift for inspiring confidence in others, and this allows them to achieve a great deal of success. They are, however, eccentric and terribly bigoted. If people dislike them, it is for this reason only. For all their patience and reticence, there is a paradoxical quality to their temperament; they anger easily and they show it. It would be wise to avoid an ox-year person when he is angry, for he is likely to do something rash to anyone confronting him. Ox-year people are mentally alert, and although they are not prone to speaking much, when required to speak they can be eloquent. They are dexterous to the point of genius and can do all sorts of things with their hands. For all their placid and easygoing ways, they are remarkably stubborn, and they hate to fail at anything they do. If they are opposed when they want to work on a project they favor, their patience may wear thin, and they can be quite unpleasant. Ox-year people regard affection between men and women as a sort of game they cannot understand, and this rather cool attitude causes their families to have difficulties with them over emotional matters.

The first phase of their life will be generally happy. The second phase will not be good; family or marital difficulties will occur, and for that period ox people will lose the respect of those who once admired them. But in their third phase of their life, whatever rough edges there might have been will be smoothed out.

Marriage for people born in the ox year is rather peculiar. The best marriages would be with persons born in either the snake year, the cock year, or the rat year; the next best, with those born in the ox, dragon, rabbit, monkey, or boar year. An ox-year person would have a bad marriage with a person born in the horse or the dog year, and the worst possible marriage would be with anyone born in the sheep year.

THE YEAR OF THE TIGER

TIGER people are sensitive, short-tempered, given to deep thinking, and capable of great sympathy for those of whom they are fond. Other people have deep respect for those born in the year of the tiger, but on occasion tiger-born people come into conflict with older people or those who have higher authority. People give tiger people much more credit for achievement than they deserve. Tiger people cannot make up their minds quickly enough and delay an important decision until it is too late to make a good one. They have somewhat narrow minds and are highly suspicious of other people and don't trust them. Although courageous and stubborn, tiger people can be selfish and just a bit mean. Yet, among Asian people, and especially the people of Japan, it is a fortuitous thing for a man to be born in the year of the tiger. The tiger, it is believed, represents the greatest terrestrial power and stands as an emblem of protection over human life. It chases away the "three disasters": thieves, fire, and ghosts.

The first and third phases of the tiger-born person's life will be smooth and easygoing. It is the second phase that will bring the most difficulties. Unless the problems during the second phase are handled carefully, they may overlap and run into the third phase.

Horse-year, dragon-year, or dog-year people make the best spouses for tiger-born people. Rat, ox, rabbit, tiger, sheep, cock, and boar are second choices. The worst marriage for a tiger-born person would be with either a snake-year or a monkey-year person.

THE YEAR OF THE RABBIT

PEOPLE born in the year of the rabbit are the most fortunate. They are smooth talkers, talented and ambitious. Virtuous and reserved, they have exceedingly fine tastes, and other people regard them with admiration and deeply trust them. Rabbit people are always financially lucky. They have a fondness for mild gossip, but they are tactful and do not speak out willingly if they have to say something bad about someone. They are very affectionate to those they love but are curiously detached from their families, regarding the other members as little better than strangers. Rabbit people have to be goaded for quite a while before they lose their tempers, for by temperament they are placid. They are very clever at business, and if someone signs a contract with a rabbit person, there can be no backing out of it.

Rabbit people are temperamentally melancholy and are able to weep at the slightest provocation. They are somewhat pedantic and not very well informed, so that, although what they know they know well, they will not seek out further information on other subjects. Rabbit people would make good gamblers, for they have the uncanny gift of picking the sure thing. They are a bit conservative and do not plunge into anything without first thinking it over carefully. Some Japanese regard rabbits with suspicion, for there is a belief that witches sometimes take the form of a rabbit. Rabbit people will have a placid existence throughout all three phases of their lives, provided they do not become involved with unmanageable elements.

Rabbit people would do well to marry persons born in either the sheep, the boar, or the dog year. A bad marriage would be with someone born in the dragon year, and the worst would be with someone from either the rat or the cock year.

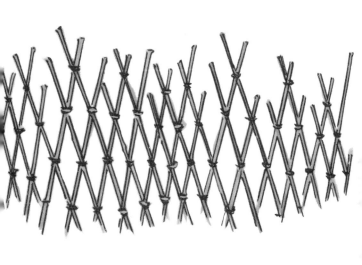

THE YEAR OF THE DRAGON

RAGON-year people are healthy and energetic and at the same time excitable, short-tempered, and terribly stubborn. These are, of course, typical attributes for the dragon-year person. However, dragon-year people are honest, sensitive, and brave and can inspire trust in almost everyone. They are the most eccentric of any in the cycle. They don't like to borrow money, or to make complimentary or flowery speeches. Yet they are sincere in what they say, and their opinions are valid. They are capable of doing good work and devoting themselves to good works. But they can be just as strong in devoting themselves to evil. They are quite softhearted and are taken in by any sort of line. This gives other people tremendous advantage over them. Dragon people worry a great deal, and for no good reason. They are not prone to marry early, and in some cases not at all. This may account for their loneliness in their old age. Yet other people love them.

Dragon-born people are somewhat fastidious. This makes it rather difficult for them in the first phase of their life. During the second phase, their fortunes will be like waves, and in the final phase, they will at last have peace and contentment. Dragon people do have big mouths and, when excited, say a great deal they don't mean, but normally they are not gossipers. Men born in the dragon year are also considered fortunate, for the dragon represents the greatest celestial power and is one of the two most beneficial astrological influences. The dragon symbolizes life and growth and is said to bring the five blessings: riches, harmony, virtue, longevity, and finishing the allotted life span.

The best marriage for the dragon-year person would be with a person born in the year of the rat, snake, monkey, or cock. Next best would be one born in the tiger, horse, sheep, or boar year. A bad marriage would be with one born in the ox, rabbit, or dragon year. The worst would be with one born in the year of the dog.

15

THE YEAR OF THE SNAKE

PEOPLE born in this year, the year of the snake, are deep. They speak very little and possess tremendous wisdom. They are unbelievably fortunate in money matters in that they never have to worry about them. They will always be able to obtain money whenever they need it. Snake-year people are quite vain and always dress up to the point of foppery. They are selfish and just a bit stingy when they are approached for a loan. Yet people born in the snake year have tremendous sympathy for others and will try to help them, much to the annoyance of those they are helping, since snake-year people habitually overdo anything they do. This cannot be helped because snake people have doubts about other people's judgment and prefer to rely on their own accumulated wisdom. They are very determined in what they do and hate to fail at anything, and although they are calm by nature, they are most intense; if they shoot an arrow at a target, they must hit that target.

People born in the snake year are quite passionate and are handsome if they are men and beauties if they are women. A compliment to a Japanese woman is to tell her that she is a *mi-bijin*, which means a snake-year beauty. However, people born in the snake year will always have marital troubles, for snake-year spouses have affections outside of the family. If they were to confine such affection to their immediate family, their lives would be much smoother. Great care must be taken in the third phase of a snake-year person's life, for it is the last phase that is the worst.

Snake-year people would be wise to marry anyone born in either the ox or the cock year. The next best marriage for them would be with those born in either the rat, rabbit, dragon, snake, horse, sheep, or dog year. A bad marriage would be with someone born in the monkey year, and the worst would be with a person born in either the tiger or the boar year.

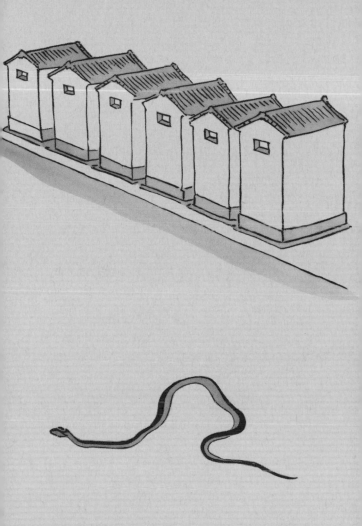

THE YEAR OF THE HORSE

HORSE-YEAR people are very skillful in paying compliments and are quite popular. They are very cheerful people, but they talk too much. They are also very skillful with money and handle finances well. They are quick in everything they do and are able to grasp other people's meanings even before these people have a chance to think out what they want to say. They are wise and talented and are good with their hands. Horse-year people are very decorative and showy in dress and manner. Although clever-looking, appearing as though they will never lose at anything they do, inside they are rather weak, especially toward members of the other sex; and if they are involved, whatever project they might be working on, they will fail at it. Horse-year people are not noted for their patience. They are hot-blooded, but in their everyday work they can be dispassionate over what they do. In their affections they are stimulated almost to the point of being blind to everything else.

Horse-year people like theatrical entertainment and always go to plays and musicals, conventions, operas— almost any place where there are entertainers and large crowds. Horse people anger quickly, and by showing their anger they lose whatever confidence people may have had in them. They are terribly independent. They will not listen to advice, and as soon as they are able, they must strike out on their own, breaking away from family influence. During the first and second phases of their life, horse people will have much trouble, but during the third phase they will have a good life.

Tiger-year, dog-year, and sheep-year people would make the best marriage for those born in the horse year. The next best would be those born in either the dragon, snake, monkey, cock, or boar year. A bad marriage for horse people would be a marriage to people born in the year of the ox, rabbit, or horse. The worst marriage would be with one born in the rat year.

18

THE YEAR OF THE SHEEP

ELEGANT, highly accomplished in the arts, passionate by nature, a person born in the sheep year would, at first glance, seem to be better off than people born in the zodiac's other years. It is not so. For people born in the year of the sheep are shy, pessimistic, puzzled about life, and uncertain over what direction they should take. Deeply religious and timid by nature—timid to the point of a woman's timidity—they are never the world's conquerors or leaders. They are clumsy in speech and make poor salesmen, yet they are passionate in whatever they do and whatever they believe in, and not just in their affections either. Because they are uncertain about themselves and what they should do, sheep people must be guided, and in this case they will be best at the arts. Throughout their whole life, people born in the sheep year will never have problems over *i-shoku-ju* (having clothes, a good table, and comfortable living), for their abilities will always make money for them so that they will always be able to exercise their good taste.

Wise and gentle in their ways, sheep people are easily stimulated to pity for those who are unfortunate. They are the sort of people who, upon hearing of a family that is destitute, will leave packages of food at their door or anonymously send them money, expecting no thanks and not wanting any. They would be too embarrassed to receive thanks. People born in the sheep year will have love and emotional problems during the second phase of their life, but during the third phase they will have extreme good fortune.

The best marriage for a sheep-year person would be with either a rabbit-year person, a boar-year person, or a person born in the year of the horse. Next best would be one born in the year of the tiger, dragon, snake, sheep, monkey, or cock. A bad marriage would be with one born in the rat year, and the worst would be with one born in either the ox or the dog year.

THE YEAR OF THE MONKEY

PEOPLE born in the year of the monkey are the erratic geniuses of the cycle. Clever and skillful in grand-scale operations, they are adroit when making financial deals. They are surprisingly inventive and original and are able to solve the most difficult problems with astonishing ease. There are few fields in which a person born in this year would not be successful. Monkey-year people have a disconcerting habit of agreeing with others. They feel more comfortable when they agree, but this sort of agreement is merely a policy tactic. If a monkey-year person sets out to do something and is unable to start immediately, he becomes discouraged and abandons the project even before he has actually tried it. Monkey people have a poor opinion of other people and tend to hold them in contempt.

Yet monkey people are prized for their skills, talents, and flexibility. They are good at making decisions and have common-sense practicality. They are fired with a deep desire for knowledge, and they read, see, and know a great deal. They have good memories and can recall fine points and details with ease. They are also passionate and strong-natured, but they tend to cool off quickly. They become famous if they are allowed to pursue their own course. Monkey people, for all their negative qualities, are needed for their skills.

The second phase in the monkey person's life is the worst, for he will be distracted and confused, and plans will go awry. The monkey-year man's relations with women will not be good. Monkey-year people must also be careful about overexplaining, for by talking too much they will drive people away.

The best marriage partner for monkey people would be someone born in the dragon or the rat year. The next best would be a person born in the year of the rabbit, sheep, or dog. A bad marriage would be one with a snake-year or a boar-year person, and the worst would be with someone born in the tiger year.

THE YEAR OF THE COCK

COCK-YEAR people are deep thinkers. They are always busy and devoted to their work. They always want to do more than they are able, and if they undertake a task beyond their abilities, they are disappointed when they discover they are unable to fulfill their obligation. People born in this year are eccentric, and it is this eccentricity that prevents them from having what is known in Japan as a "roundness" in their relationships with others. Cock people always think that they are right and that they know what they are doing. They do not trust other people and prefer to do what they like, alone. Their outward attitude and presentation is that of an adventuresome spirit, but inwardly they have little gift for high adventure and are filled with nonsensical plans that never mature.

Although they are ambitious, for all their deep thinking they are not far-seeing and are somewhat improvident, for their fortunes resemble waves: sometimes they are wealthy, sometimes not. They are selfish and unheeding of other people's feelings and have a habit of speaking out directly whenever they have something on their minds. They are not at all shy and are quite brave when the occasion calls for it. Other people find cock people interesting, but unless they are careful, cock people will lose the good opinion of others.

The best marriage for this sort of person is with either ox-year, snake-year, or dragon-year people. The next best would be with someone born in the year of the tiger, horse, sheep, monkey, or boar. A bad marriage would be with someone born in the rat year, cock year, or dog year. The worst marriage would be with someone born in the year of the rabbit.

THE YEAR OF THE DOG

ALL the fine traits of human nature are in the possession of people born in the year of the dog. They have a deep sense of duty and loyalty, are extremely honest, and always do their best in their relationships with people. Dog-year people inspire other people's confidence and know how to keep private secrets absolutely private. Other people hold dog-year people in high regard and consider them fine persons. Yet dog-year people are somewhat selfish, terribly stubborn, and exceedingly eccentric. They care little for wealth yet always seem to manage to obtain money when they need it. They are not good at social gatherings, and emotionally they are cold. If there is any worst trait about these people it is their ability to find fault with things and their caustic remarks criticizing what they think wrong. They have terribly sharp tongues.

It will be noted that throughout history it has always been a person who was born in the year of the dog who has been the champion of justice. Goaded by whatever injustice he may see, a dog-year person will not rest until right has been established. Eccentric as he is, he does not champion stupid causes, which is a good thing after all, for when a dog-year person takes up a cause he generally sees it through, and the side he takes up wins. Dog people are not noted for small talk, yet they make good leaders in industry. They are able to handle people when it is necessary, and trading firms or big business firms would be wise to hire such people for their industriousness and honesty.

Surprisingly, for all the dog-year person's cool temperament, marriage with either horse-year, tiger-year, or rabbit-year people would be best. Next best would be marriage with a person born in the year of the rat, snake, monkey, dog, or boar. A bad marriage would be one with someone born in the year of the ox or the year of the cock. The worst would be with someone born in either the dragon year or the sheep year.

THE YEAR OF THE BOAR

C HIVALROUS and gallant, people born in the year of the boar are always flying the white banner of purity. Whatever their ambition, they do what they must with all the strength they have, for their strength is an inner strength that no one can overcome. There is neither left nor right nor retreat when a boar person sets out to do something. He has tremendous fortitude and great honesty.

Boar-year people don't make many friends, but when they do, they make friends for life, and anyone having a boar-year-born person as a friend is indeed fortunate. Boar-year people don't talk much, but when they finally say something, they let it all come out at one time, and there is no shutting them up until they have finished. Like monkey-year people, they have a great thirst for knowledge. They study a great deal and on the surface are generally well informed. However, if a boar person's knowledge is probed, it will be discovered that what he knows is limited. The Japanese saying is that such a person is broad in front but has a narrow back.

Boar people are quite short-tempered, yet they hate quarreling or arguments. They are affectionate and kind to their loved ones. Boar people will have marital problems, and during the first and second phases of their lives they will have difficulties. Yet no matter how difficult their problems may be, boar people are shy and will not ask for outside help but will seek solutions to their problems by themselves. Boar people are advised not to get into lawsuits, for, being impulsive and honest, they will lose the suit to someone who is unscrupulous.

Rabbit and sheep people make the best spouses for those born in the year of the boar. The next best choice of a spouse would be any of those born in the rat, ox, tiger, dragon, horse, cock, or dog year. A bad marriage would be with one born in either the monkey or the boar year, and the worst person to marry would be someone born in the year of the snake.

RAT 子	1972 1984 1996 2008 2020 2032	HORSE 午	1 1 2 2 2 2
OX 丑	1973 1985 1997 2009 2021 2033	SHEEP 未	1 1 2 2 2 2
TIGER 寅	1974 1986 1998 2010 2022 2034	MONKEY 申	1 1 2 2 2 2
RABBIT 卯	1975 1987 1999 2011 2023 2035	COCK 酉	1 1 2 2 2 2
DRAGON 辰	1976 1988 2000 2012 2024 2036	DOG 戌	1 1 2 2 2 2
SNAKE 巳	1977 1989 2001 2013 2025 2037	BOAR 亥	2 2 2 2 2